Cat Files

Lion

WRITTEN BY
BETHANY LATHAM

KidHaven
PUBLISHING

Published in 2027 by
KidHaven Publishing, an Imprint of Greenhaven Publishing, LLC
2544 Clinton St., Buffalo, NY 14224

Written by: Bethany Latham
Edited by: Rebecca Phillips-Bartlett
Designed by: Ker Ker Lee

Cataloging-in-Publication Data
Names: Latham, Bethany.
Title: Lion / Bethany Latham.
Description: Buffalo, NY : KidHaven Publishing, 2027. | Series: Cat files | Includes glossary and index.
Identifiers: ISBN 9781534569591 (pbk.) | ISBN 9781534569607 (library bound) | ISBN 9781534569614 (ebook)
Subjects: LCSH: Lion--Juvenile literature. | Lion--Behavior--Juvenile literature.
Classification: LCC QL737.C23 L384 2027 | DDC 599.757--dc23

Printed in China

CPSIA compliance information: Batch #QS27KH: For further information contact Greenhaven Publishing LLC at 1-844-317-7404.

Please visit our website, www.greenhavenpublishing.com. For a free color catalog of all our high-quality books, call toll free 1-844-317-7404 or fax 1-844-317-7405.

Find us on

Photo Credits – Images courtesy of Shutterstock.com, unless otherwise stated.

Cover & Recurring – Eric Isselee, Maksim Nafikov, AminaStock, BMR Creation, graficriver_icons_logo, Vector Tradition, Maggy Meyer. 2–3 – Dr Ajay Kumar Singh. 4–5 – Rudi Hulshof, Mousam Ray, Sagephotography.in, Gunter Nuyts. 6–7 – Seyms Brugger, Jrossphoto. 8–9 – Simon Dannhauer, Andrea Chiozzi. 10–11 – Eric Isselee, Rudi Hulshof, Morozova Olgal. 12–13 – SRI EKAWATI WIJAYANTI, Alta Oosthuizen, BMR Creation. 14–15 – Abhiraj Palakkattel, Rudi Hulshof. 16–17 – Henrico Muller, Gunter Nuyts. 18–19 – Richard Juilliart, Andrea Chiozzi. 20–21 – TODD17, Ondrej Prosicky. 22–23 – G and T Adventures, Manoj Kumar Tuteja.

Contents

Words that look like <u>this</u> can be found in the glossary on page 24.

Big Cats

Big cats are carnivorous predators. Carnivores eat meat. Predators hunt the animals they eat. Scientists group big cats together because they have a lot in common. Most big cats have sharp claws and large, strong teeth.

Lion

Cheetah

Big cats are a special group of cats that includes lions, tigers, and snow leopards. Other large cats, such as cheetahs, may seem like big cats, but they are part of a different group.

FACT FILE

DIET:	Carnivore
ANIMAL TYPE:	Mammal
HUNTING:	Predator

Lions

Lions are the second largest big cat. They are mostly found in sub-Saharan Africa. This means they live in countries below the Sahara, which is a desert. Male lions are best known for their large manes.

Some lions also live in India.

FACT FILE

CONTINENT:	Africa and Asia
SIZE:	Around 10 feet (3 m) long (without tail)
WEIGHT:	Usually between 278 and 419 pounds (126 and 190 kg)
SPEED:	Up to 50 miles (80 km) per hour

Habitat

An animal's habitat is its natural home. Lions usually live on savannas or in open woodlands. Savannas are large, flat grasslands with a few plants and trees. Lions can adapt to many places but are not usually found in rainforests or deserts.

Lions need lots of prey to eat. This makes the savanna a great home for lions. Many large plant-eating animals, or herbivores, live on the savanna. Lions hunt and eat the herbivores.

Savannas have only two seasons—wet and dry.

Body

Lions all have these important body parts:

Lions have yellow, gold, brown, or tawny fur.

Only male lions have a mane.

Male lion

Lions have long and powerful teeth.

Lions' paws are large and strong.

Female lion

A lion's body is strong and powerful.

Lions' tails have a darker tuft at the end.

Lions' claws are long and sharp.

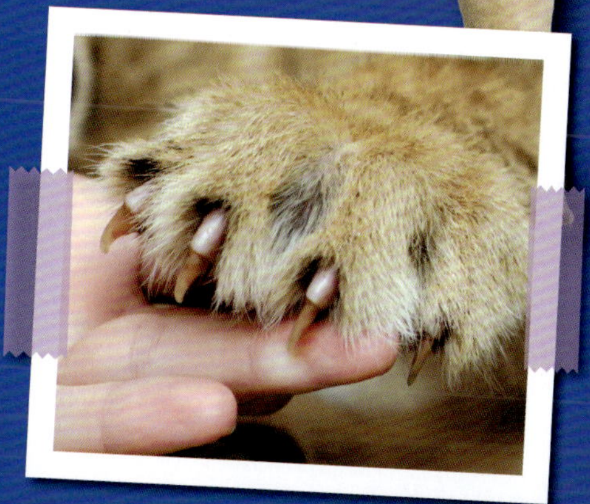

Lions have short, strong legs.

Blending In

The color of a lion's fur helps it camouflage itself. The lion blends in with the grass, which makes it hard to spot. This type of camouflage is called concealing coloration.

Lions have fixed camouflage because their fur does not change color.

FACT FILE

COLOR:	Yellow
PATTERN:	Plain
FUR LENGTH:	Short
CAMOUFLAGE TYPE:	Concealing and fixed

Lions use grass and bushes for cover when hunting. Female lions, or lionesses, blend in better because they do not have manes. Lionesses do most of the hunting because of this.

Hunting Prey

Lionesses do most of the hunting. They are more agile and better camouflaged than males. Lions often hunt in pairs or small groups. Lions eat large herbivores, such as buffalo, zebras, and wildebeests.

Lions suffocate their prey by biting its neck or nose.

Lions usually hunt when it is dark so that they are harder to spot. Lions hunt by stalking their prey, meaning they follow it very quietly.

FACT FILE

CLAW LENGTH: Around 1.2 inches (3 cm)

TEETH LENGTH: Up to 2.8 inches (7 cm)

FOOD EATEN: 11 to 22 pounds (5 to 10 kg) a day

Family Life

Lions are the only big cats that live in groups. A group of lions is called a pride. There can be as many as 40 lions in one pride. Usually there are around 15.

Prides roar together. Their roars can be heard 5 miles (8 km) away.

Most of the lions in a pride are female. They are usually family members. There are often one to six males in a pride. Young males leave their pride when they are two to four years old.

FACT FILE

GROUP NAME:	Pride
GROUP SIZE:	Up to 40
COMMUNICATION:	Roaring

Raising Young

Young lions are called cubs. A mother is usually pregnant for around three months. She usually has two to four cubs. Some lionesses have up to six cubs at once.

Cubs have spots. The spots fade as the cubs grow up.

FACT FILE

NAME:	Cub
NUMBER:	Usually two to four
PREGNANCY LENGTH:	Around three months
WHEN FULLY GROWN:	Three years

The lionesses in a pride often have cubs at the same time. Cubs get milk from other lionesses as well as their mother.

Cats in Danger

Scientists label lions as vulnerable. This means the number of lions in the wild is falling. Lions have fewer wild places and animals to hunt because humans are farming more. Humans also hunt lions' prey.

Trophy hunters kill lions for their body parts. Trophy hunting is allowed in some African countries. However, many other African countries have banned trophy hunting. They are trying to protect lions.

Cat Files

Lions are truly impressive big cats. They are fierce hunters and very family focused. Do you think you would like to see a lion in the wild?

Roar-Some Roundup

CONTINENT:	Africa and Asia
HABITAT:	Grasslands and woodlands
FUR LENGTH:	Short
GROUP NAME:	Pride
GROUP SIZE:	Up to 40

Big cats are amazing animals that need protecting. You can do some research with a grown-up about how to help lions!

Glossary

adapt change over time to suit the environment

agile able to move quickly and easily

camouflage to hide by blending into the surroundings

mammal an animal that is warm-blooded, has a backbone, and makes milk to feed its young

pregnant when a female animal has one or more babies growing inside her

prey animals that are hunted by other animals for food

suffocate to die from not having enough air to breathe

trophy hunters people who hunt animals for enjoyment or sport, not for food, and often display the animals they kill

tuft a bunch of hair that grows closely together

Index